The Say and Duck Chronicles
Part 1

By

Barbara J. Belisle

ISBN: 1-4140-0273-4 (e-book)
ISBN: 1-4140-0309-9 (Paperback)

Library of Congress Control Number: 2003096315

This book is printed on acid free paper.

Printed in the United States of America
Bloomington, IN

1stBooks - rev. 11/11/03

DEDICATION

This book is dedicated to my family who constantly said, "Do it!" Their support and patience are rewards that I add to the many blessings I have received through them.

TABLE OF CONTENTS

MANNERS 1

THE WORST KIND 3

UGH!! 5

PATIENT CARE 7

HUH? 9

T.V. AND KIDS 11

LOWER THAN LOW 13

THE NRA 15

UGH!! 17

CORRECTLY SPEAKING 19

TRASH EFFECTS 21

ABORTION 23

READER? REPORTER? 27

NOT GUILTY? 29

WHERE? 31

NO ALLEGIANCE 33

POLITICAL AFFAIRS 35

THE CONFEDERATE FLAG 37

AFFIRMATIVE ACTION 43

POOR GRAMMAR USAGE 47

LEAD US NOT 49

TRASH EFFECTS 51

HOMOSEXUALS 53

SAVE THE TREES 55

MORALITY 57

BIGOTS 63

RUNNING 67

SMOKERS' CHOICE 69

PUBLIC SCHOOL CRITICS 71

UN-RAP! 73

SWEEPSTAKES 75

BAGGY CLOTHES 77

E-MAILERS 79

HUMAN CARE 81

WIMP—ETTE 83

A CALL FOR POCKETS 85

CHRISTIANITY 87

HUH? 89

THE UNTRAINED 93

WHAT I CALL GOOD TV 95

THE TEN COMMANDMENTS 97

LAND 99

ABOUT THE AUTHOR 101

MANNERS

Doesn't anybody teach children manners anymore? Do people even know there are such things as manners? A young man entered the building where I work, and he removed his hat immediately. I was so surprised that I called him over, asked him if I could get a hug, and though in shock because he didn't know me, he said, "Yes Ma'am." Then I explained to him how good it was to see a well-mannered young man remove his hat when he entered a building. Who told men it was ok to keep hats on in buildings? Their lives won't come to an end if they don't remove them, but if they do, it's a sign that they're cultured and respectful of others.

I have watched people bump into each other or one steps on the other's foot accidentally, and neither one says, "Excuse me." I've seen and heard people pass gas and laugh as if nothing happened. The same is true of loud belching. And when will some people learn not to talk and chew with food in their mouths.? I've also observed that many people don't know how to use a knife and fork. To cut their food, they hold their eating utensils as if they're attacking it. A little instruction and practice can easily correct that. Exhibiting proper conduct always creates a positive image.

The same is true of men walking on the outside when walking down the street with a lady, assisting a lady stepping off the curb, entering and exiting a car, and holding a lady's chair as she sits down at a table. Where is that good old chivalric behavior?

Where is lady-like behavior? Some girls are as loud and uncouth as some men. They pass gas out loud and laugh, they belch at the table, and they even say things like, "I've got to go pee," in mixed (males and females) company without even batting an eye. If women don't demand respect and act respectfully, they will never have the high regard they deserve.

Good manners never hurt anyone; actually, they attract people with class.

THE WORST KIND

Anyone who molests a child is the crud left over after manure dries up. Like crud, the molester should be bagged and crushed in a garbage truck.

Barbara J. Belisle

UGH!!

Women who fight over "men" on talk shows should have their heads examined. The "men" they fight over look like illiterate punks who can't read or write a decent paragraph and wouldn't know how to spell a word if it wasn't tattooed on their arms.

Barbara J. Belisle

PATIENT CARE

How can an insurance company (or some other type of profit—oriented group) tell a doctor how to treat a patient or what to treat or not treat??

Barbara J. Belisle

HUH?

Some interviewers ask the dumbest questions. Perhaps you've seen some of our "star" anchors and reporters ask victims of tornadoes who have lost everything, "How did you feel when you saw that your home was totally destroyed?" Or you've heard the very profound, "What was it like to hear that your son was one of the ones assumed dead in the rubble of the WTC?" If one is not mature enough or intelligent enough to handle a thorough and responsible interview, then let someone else do it, or don't do it at all.

Barbara J. Belisle

T.V. AND KIDS

There is a group of people who write, produce, direct, act in, and / or sponsor material that is vulgar, crass, violent, gross, and uncouth, and they think most people appreciate it. They also think that what they "present" to us, even in "cute" animation form, is fine for the young people as well. These people also want the public to believe that children speak vulgarly to their parents and their teachers, everybody uses the "F" word, sexual activity is rampant (and always occurs on the first date), and being ill-mannered and disrespectful is the norm. Well, I'm here to tell them they're wrong. Most people don't appreciate this crap, and most people are angry because of the negative influence this type of material has had on the young people. I truly believe that there are some subversives who hate loving families, good kids, and wholesomeness, in general, mainly because they never experienced those qualities in their lives. Using freedom of speech as justification for their depictions, they wave the Constitution "flag" to cover their tracks. Sure, they have a right to write, produce, and present the filth, but they ought to have sense enough to say to themselves, "This material won't be beneficial to anybody, and certainly not to young people. Let's see if we can change that a little." In other words, don't embellish, add to, promote, or intensify the problem. Instead, try to portray morally upright situations that emphasize proper behavior and teach lessons people can live by.

LOWER THAN LOW

Any female who takes her clothes off to "dance" vulgarly or to perform sexual acts in person or on camera to entertain men (or anybody) belittles herself and becomes the symbol of filth and deviance required of perverts, misfits, and clammy sickos. No amount of money should entice anyone to stoop that low.

Barbara J. Belisle

THE NRA

The NRA should be shot!! This group of reprobates is responsible for the proliferation of guns and heavy weapons all over this country. They are responsible for all the weapons in the hands of the secret paramilitary groups who are planning a race war in this country, the Black hoodlums who are dealing drugs, gangbanging, and having drive-bys, the skinheads and Aryan nation sickies, and the decent, law-abiding citizens who occasionally crack up and blow somebody away, or their children get hold of the gun(s) and kill somebody who hurt their feelings. Just because the Bill of Rights states that we all have the right to bear arms, the men who wrote it didn't have in mind the advanced weaponry we have today nor the murders and killings that have been common in our society. They lived in a different time when British soldiers were likely to be in their homes and on their streets by order of the king and not because the colonists wanted them there.

If the NRA would get out of the pockets of the financial backers of certain politicians and the "men" who hate Bill Clinton and become real men and women again, they'll praise the technology that could protect not only children from accidentally firing a weapon but grownups as well. They'll be thankful that some drunken wacko or hatemonger can't buy a gun at a gun show. They'll be grateful that their wives and daughters and sons got to their cars or doors to their houses without being shot by some idiot who wanted their vehicle or their money. Each night when they lie down in bed, they can reflect on another day without a child being killed by a gun and think, "I helped to make that possible." Stop singing those same old songs, "Apply the laws already on the books," "Guns don't kill people...," and "...right to bear arms." Sing instead, "Tossing the NRA away; we're Nice, Responsible Americans today."

UGH!!

Wedgies look nasty. Increase pants size.

Barbara J. Belisle

CORRECTLY SPEAKING

The English teacher in most middle schools and high schools has not had English grammar since middle school and high school, so he/she doesn't know it. Also, there was a time when teachers required students to speak correctly at all times. If a student were walking in the hall, and the teacher heard someone say something incorrectly, the teacher stopped the student and asked him / her to "Say that again, correctly." Not anymore. The "fad" today is, "I'm not grading for mechanics (correct usage), only contents." Well, no wonder people are going around saying things like, "If I would have…"

Remember the movement to make English the national language, and all immigrants coming here would be required to speak it? All written forms such as applications, driving tests, sales slips, etc. would be in English. I do believe that people who choose to live in America should be able to speak English, but Americans should be required to know it as well.

TRASH EFFECTS

Certain types of talk shows should be forbidden—by law! Guests from dysfunctional families and those who are too illiterate to understand that they're being used to increase ratings and pocketbooks are told, in many cases, how to react and, if necessary, to enhance their stories for applause. These poor people leave the shows to go back to who knows what, while the hosts ride off in their limousines counting their dollars.

Barbara J. Belisle

ABORTION

When a woman gets pregnant, she's either happy or sad about it. If her station in life is a happy one, then all is well. But if a woman's husband is an idiot who raises hell every day, or he beats her whenever he gets drunk or just feels like it, and he rapes her and does terrible things to her, why, in the name of all that is good and decent, would she want to carry then bear his child? A young girl who gets pregnant has no business with a baby. In most cases, her mother ends up raising the child anyway. The point is, who has the right to tell a woman that she has to have the baby-whether she wants it or not? If she doesn't have to use the taxpayers' money, then the decision is hers alone.

Those people who protest around abortion clinics and offices of doctors who perform abortions should realize that just because they think it's wrong doesn't mean they have the right to push their beliefs on others. Each individual must live his / her life as he /she sees fit, as long as it doesn't infringe upon the life of someone else. Each individual will have to answer to his / her God in due time. A woman who is pregnant with an unwanted child wrestles within her heart and mind about the action she will take, and I'm sure she prays for her God's understanding and forgiveness. No one can know what is in her heart, and no one has the right to force her into doing something she doesn't want to. Also, no man can tell a woman what she should do about her pregnancy. He doesn't have to carry the baby in his body for nine months, suffering all the various ailments that accompany pregnancies, nor does he have to suffer the pain and misery of childbirth. Then, in many cases, after the baby comes, he's not there to help with the child. But that's another story.

Having a child is a beautiful event in any family, but if the situation is a miserable one, it will also be bad for the child. If a woman makes up her mind to have an abortion, the sooner she does it, the better. To wait four or more months causes an attachment / bonding that will make it too painful mentally, emotionally, and, to me, morally as well. If women, and young ladies who have not chosen abstinence, would take the pill and, if possible, insist on precautions from male companions, then there would be no need for abortions. But a lot of women are in situations that they didn't intend to be in, and they get pregnant when they don't want to be. Whatever they decide to do about their condition is their business—and no one else's.

Barbara J. Belisle

READER? REPORTER?

Journalist? Reporter? Anchorperson? Researcher? Writer? Reader? If one can read with expression and has "the look," can he / she become a star? Then why the competition for ratings? The ones who go out into the field of action and reports from the site gets my praise.

Barbara J. Belisle

NOT GUILTY?

I have never been able to understand how a defendant can be found "Not Guilty" when he / she actually committed the crime. In the case where a young Japanese student was shot to death when he knocked on the door of a house in a Southern state, the man of the house did shoot the young man, but he was found not guilty during the trial. Can you imagine how the parents of that young man felt when they heard that verdict? How could the man be found not guilty if he actually shot the young man? He did it, didn't he?

Barbara J. Belisle

WHERE?

Geography should be required in ninth grade and again in twelfth grade so that students will be able to find places on a world map without gaping in ignorance.

Barbara J. Belisle

NO ALLEGIANCE

Owners of companies that put Americans out of work by moving out of the country for cheaper labor should be labeled as traitors. It is sinful to place money in a higher position of importance than people. Instead of coming up with pretty words like "downsizing", try words like "trainassign" which means "train and reassign". If there is enough money to build a new company in another country, can't it be used to make sure employees don't lose their jobs in this one? Taking away a family's livelihood has a devastating effect on its members; those who cause that devastation can't be called loyal American citizens.

Barbara J. Belisle

POLITICAL AFFAIRS

Bill and Hillary Clinton could have made a lot of positive changes in this great country if their enemies had left them alone. His affair with Monica should have been left to him, Hillary, and God. Many presidents have had affairs. Many politicians have had affairs (and are still having them). To try to punish the President because he had an affair and tried to hide the fact is ridiculous. I personally believe that the incident that should have required punishment, even prison time, for those involved was the arms deal with Iran. Remember?

NOTE:I thought basketball season ended in early spring—before baseball season.

THE CONFEDERATE FLAG

The "flag flap" is about racists who can't stand seeing black people improving their lives—some doing better than they are. They see black people only as the stereotypes portrayed in Hollywood's pimp movies and television's sex-crazed, ebonics-talking, exaggerated characters in non-realistic situation comedies. They don't know that most Blacks are hard-working, decent, church-going people who have the same hopes and dreams that white people do. These racists use the Confederate flag as a means to flaunt their hatred. They know that, and so do black people. Shoot, half of them not only don't know the history of the Civil War, they can't even spell Confederate.

There's nothing wrong with honoring one's heritage and memorializing ancestors who fought and died in the war; that's what museums and archives are for. Think about all the people who died in the War of 1812, World War I, World War II, the Korean War, and Vietnam. Museums and memorials have been established to remember those brave souls. Americans show their respect and gratefulness to these fallen heroes in many ways, but these celebrations and memorials are not divisive; all Americans are welcome to participate. The American flag that is flown during these ceremonies represents all Americans.

The Confederate flag represents division. It represents a "nation" that broke away from the United States and fought a war to stay that way in order to maintain their way of life and to keep Blacks enslaved. That "nation" lost the war. It is a part of the UNITED States again. The American flag flies proudly over all of America's capitol buildings representing ALL of the people. Those who want to fly other flags that cause dissension and bitterness among America's citizens should consider leaving this country and starting your own somewhere else, then they can fly their flag over their capitol building and any other building they want to.

There was a time when I use to say that the "flag flap" could be easily settled. The racists who want their Confederate flag to fly above the Capitol could be satisfied by having it fly on a pole on one side of the pole that holds the American flag, while the red, black, and green Black Americans' flag can fly on a pole on the opposite side of the American flag. (Of course, the flags would be the same size and rise the same height up the pole.) But, that represents divisiveness also.

Barbara J. Belisle

NOTE:I wish someone would tell drivers who put their blinkers on because the driver in front of them is turning to study the driver's manual again. Leave blinkers off if not turning!!

NOTE: I do not understand how a criminal can be sent to jail or prison and still be able to rape another prisoner. Where are the guards? If the guards can't guard, get rid of them.

Barbara J. Belisle

AFFIRMATIVE ACTION

The first slaves were brought to America in 1619. The Emancipation Proclamation was enacted in 1863. Jim Crow laws were adopted around 1896, and the "separate but equal" policy, in reality, turned out to be "separate and inferior." The Civil Rights movement lasted from Linda Brown in the '50's to around 1968 with the Civil Rights Act. Eventually, the idea of affirmative action began to spread around the country guaranteeing that so many Blacks would be hired or enrolled in various institutions and / or corporations. (I can attest to the "token Black' experience.) Knowing that there are still white separatists who own corporations and head colleges and institutions, some political leaders and other bigots want to eliminate affirmative action because (they say) it's unfair to white folks. They must be crazy! Just like racist bigots blame their failures on Black

43

people, those who claim they're not racist say they just want to be fair. If that's the case, then do your math. For 380 years, Blacks have been enslaved in America in one form or another. Affirmative action has been in effect for about thirty years. Can anyone out there tell me what's wrong with this picture?

NOTE: One moment of peace and contentment, though brief, can be uplifting and a standard by which we judge other accomplishments during a day.

NOTE: Stupid people don't know they're stupid.

POOR GRAMMAR USAGE

Poor grammar students are now writing books, articles, commercials, scripts, and songs. They're adding S's to words that are already plural, such as "women," "men" "children," and "people." They're misusing "you're," which sounds like u're, and means "you are" and "your," which rhymes with "door," and shows possession or ownership. Though "here's" and "there's" are singular and can only refer to one thing, ('s means is) they're used to refer to more than one thing. Pronouns that follow prepositions are usually incorrect, such as "between him and I", etc. "Be sure and" and "try and" have become so common, it's puke-provoking. I'm going to write a little handbook for easy reference to try TO correct some of the regularly used errors. I think I'll call it, "Where's U're?"

NOTE: Common courtesy is becoming rarer and rarer. If we can flood the market with everything else, why not this?

LEAD US NOT

How did school prayer become an issue? What's wrong with praying in school and in the car while driving down the highway or in the grocery store or on a ferris wheel? I've always prayed—everywhere—silently. God didn't ask us to pray out loud in a group. He knows that many people are hypocrites who will put on a front while in a group praying, then they'll turn around and curse somebody out or burn a cross while peering through the holes of a white sheet that covers his/her face. Just because one prays in a group doesn't mean anything if he/she isn't pure in heart. In a place of worship, group prayer is fine, but in social gatherings, a moment of silent meditation or reflection is appropriate. So, what's the big deal?

NOTE: If I were a man who is healthy and not past middle age, I wouldn't want anyone to know I needed Viagra.

TRASH EFFECTS

The ads in some magazines are obviously meant to satisfy voyeurs who get their "kicks" from viewing women who have dresses raised or are transparent and hanging off breasts and bottoms. Some pictures even show girls curled up with other girls, men touching or nearly touching private parts of girls or other boys, and suggestive poses that don't leave anything for the imagination—all just to sell perfume or a purse or a piece of clothing. These types of ads appear in magazines intended for young women and girls who, of course, will be influenced by what they see. A reputable magazine would not contain this kind of junk. Let the sickos get their thrills from the "rags" published in the darkened hole-in-the-walls that smell of filth and reek with the muck they desire.

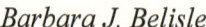

NOTE:Bigots are sexually incompetent. No wonder their stupidity
   rules.

HOMOSEXUALS

Who cares whether or not a person is a homosexual? I don't—as long as he / she keeps it private. Nobody needs to know what consenting adults do behind closed doors, but flaunting the fact and demanding equality and legal status are unacceptable aspects of the issue. There have always been homosexuals—some historically famous. There are millions of them today—some we wouldn't even think were, but they keep their "business" to themselves. And there will always be homosexuals. They have a right to exist peacefully just like anybody else, and their salvation and/or damnation will be determined by God and not by some holier-than-thou individual whose own salvation is in doubt.

NOTE: There's something to be said to the young woman who thinks breast implants are necessary to be noticed, accepted, or dated; poor thing!

SAVE THE TREES

Trees hold moisture, provide shade, furnish homes for all kinds of animals, keep us cool with their breezes, and aid in the production of rain. Why doesn't our government forbid developers from cutting them down to build subdivisions, malls, service stations, and quick marts? Why can't they build within the trees and / or re-plant what has to be cut down? Better yet, why don't the developers become innovative and refurbish all of those wonderful old buildings in downtown urban areas and plant trees to beautify? Not only can they create condos for the upwardly mobiles and senior citizens who want secure-living facilities, but they can also get homeless people off the streets by creating self sufficient housing units out of the vacant military buildings sitting unused on closed bases around the country. Unless something is done to SAVE THE TREES, temperatures are going to continue to rise, droughts will be longer and worst, animals will die needlessly on highways seeking shelter and food, and many people will suffer from excessive heat, food shortages, and increased homelessness. Demand that developers THINK before they cut.

Oops! They (?) have just cut down the last of the grand, old trees that stood on the grounds of the high school here in town. When they (?) cut down all the beautiful old oaks that lined the sidewalks around the school a few years ago, so many of us cried and complained, that we never thought that it could happen again. How wrong we were! Now that beautiful old school looks like a box lying in the middle of a football field. Idiots!!

MORALITY

Who told the Republicans they had dibs on morality and family values? Most people, regardless of race, nationality, or religion, are brought up by moral people who try to instill values that are godly and honorable. Most people want the perfect family, headed by a mother and father. But, life happens, and things don't always happen the way people want them to. Today, many young people, both black and white, are brought up in homes without having both parents and in which the televisions and play stations are the babysitters and nannies. Some children are affected negatively by what they see, but most are not and are growing up to be moral and upright; the families' politics are not the determinant factors. Morality and family values aren't just applicable to the Republicans nor the Democrats or Independents.

During the Monica/Bill debacle, the Republicans made it sound like no other president had had affairs or lied while in office. Congressmen in both parties have had and are having affairs. Church leaders and school presidents have had and are having affairs. People in all walks of life are doing things behind closed doors and "fronting" on the outside making people think they're upright and decent, when all the time they're nothing but hypocrites. But, just as there are immoral people who try to keep others thinking they're moral, there are moral people who are moral outside and behind closed doors.

Politics have become so immoral, it doesn't even matter whether one votes or not. The candidates are bought and paid for, and the one with the most financial backing wins. Even poll results are announced early and regularly to effect voters' choices. Long before voting booths close, results are announced on the air—affecting voter turn out in other time zones, and all in the name of ratings. It's unfair to the regular people who still believe their ballots count. It's immoral, because it smells of money. It's gotten so bad that some offices are filled with fewer than half the eligible voters casting a ballot. Congressmen are in a position to make things better in society, yet, because someone is paying them off or expecting a favor, new rulings and laws remain stagnant and eventually die. It's immoral to be in a position to improve the lives of the people but choose not to because someone told them not to—just to hurt another group or person. When will one of them stand up and say, "Forget parties, and do the right thing. This ruling will benefit us all." When will someone stand up and be moral?

NOTE:Drivers who tailgate are stupid. Ask them.

NOTE:No reputable company or organization should sponsor a show
or program that uses vulgarities and other filth to get its point
across.

Barbara J. Belisle

BIGOTS

I hate bigots! I hate stupidity! I hate bigots because they're stupid. Bigots think they're superior to minorities, especially black people. They're too dumb to realize that God created us all, and according to the cute lil' adage, "God don't (sic.) make no (sic.) junk." They're too stupid to realize that God gave us all five senses, four limbs, the same innards, the same reproductive organs, and the same method for us all to be conceived and born. We all need the same basic things to survive: air, water, food, heat when it's cold, and coolness when it's hot. We all can die of the same diseases and accidents, and none of us have long life expectances. If we're all put in similar environments, we'll all develop mentally, intellectually, socially, etc. basically the same, unless there are birth defects or accidents that stifle us. I think that one reason white people fought

63

integration so long was because they didn't want black people to know they had dumb white folks. I taught in white high schools in Alabama for almost thirty years, and I can tell you, there were black and white dumb students and black and white smart ones. The bigots I met during that time learned that love, respect, and kindness elevated their spirits, enhanced their senses (especially the "common" one), and made them realize that bigotry is stupid!

NOTE: It's ok to be thin, but skeletal? See a doctor!!!!

Barbara J. Belisle

RUNNING

(For Office)

It's a shame that a person can't run for national political office without having millions of dollars backing him/her. Integrity, experience, and nobility of ideas and plans should be the foremost qualifications demanded of any candidate. No candidate should be in the pocket of any one person or group. If he or she hasn't been bought, then his or her discussions, arguments, and voting can be based on what is good, right, and moral.

There was a time when a candidate presented a platform based on what he/she truly believed, even if some of the ideas were the same as the opponent's. Voters decided on a candidate whose views and plans most coincided with their own. Of course, personality, carriage, sense of humor, and appearance meant a little also, but at least the voters knew the candidate wasn't bought and paid for.

Today, a candidate is told what the platform is, and if a candidate doesn't want to accept it, then he/she shouldn't even bother expecting to be backed by the party. What the candidate truly believes doesn't matter; if financial backing is needed, then the candidate must do what the party wants. Can you imagine what the country would be like if the President of the United States and/or the majority party in congress voted for or against an issue based on the desires of the person or group who bought him/her?

SMOKERS' CHOICE

Why should a grown person be ordered financially rewarded if he / she CHOOSES to smoke and becomes ill because of it—KNOWING that cigarettes are harmful to one's health? (That fact is even printed on each pack.)

Barbara J. Belisle

PUBLIC SCHOOL CRITICS

Did you ever wonder who the public school critics are? They're public school graduates who turned out just fine. When schools were integrated, they suddenly had to have a reason to take their kids out of those schools, so they found fault with them. Now that they have found their academies and church schools, they're acting like public schools are so bad. Sure, there are some systems, rural and urban, that have different types of problems that are detrimental to the student body, but most public schools have outstanding curriculums, fantastic teachers who work hard to help students, and administrators who work with the teachers and give them favorable conditions in which to work.

To further cast a negative image on public schools, advocates of the school voucher are busy at work trying to get federal tax dollars to help them send their kids to segregated private schools, academies, "Christian" schools, and home schools. Sure, some of these advocates say the vouchers will benefit poor minority students who wish to transfer to "better" schools, but tell me, how many of those poor, minority students can get to those "better" schools? Can those poor, minority students dress like the "other" kids? Will those poor, minority students have money to pay for tutors? Get real!

UN-RAP!

I watched in disbelief, shock, and total disgust the profoundly negative effect that rap had on our kids.

Barbara J. Belisle

SWEEPSTAKES

It ought to be against the law for anyone or any group to have a sweepstakes if he/she or they don't have the money to pay the winner in full immediately. Why have one if you have to pay part of it now, another part in installments for twenty years? To me, that tactic seems like a scam. Then, to save their skins, they have the "winner" sign a form promising not to discuss the conditions of the transaction, or they'll forfeit the "win." To pay a person his or her winnings over a twenty year period is sinful! Give the winners their money immediately, so they can do things before they die—or don't have the sweepstakes!!

Barbara J. Belisle

BAGGY CLOTHES

I'll be so glad when grown men pull up their big, baggy pants and get rid of those big, over-large coats and jackets. I know children go through phases and fads, but men are suppose to grow beyond them.

Barbara J. Belisle

E-MAILERS

Be careful e-mailers; your ignorance of correct grammar and punctuation is showing.

Barbara J. Belisle

HUMAN CARE

No medicine should cost more than the average person can afford. No human being should have to choose either medicine or food because of the cost. The people who develop and sell the different kinds of medicines should realize they're human also and have no special formula to cure any terminal illness they might get or that will give them life forever. To profit from people's sickness or from their need to have warmth or freeze to death (as with the gas and electric companies) because of greed is not only sinful but also criminal and treasonous.

Barbara J. Belisle

WIMP—ETTE

A man who beats his wife or any woman is not a man; he's a piece of crud who has been pissed on by somebody he was too scared to face.

Barbara J. Belisle

A CALL FOR POCKETS

Will someone please tell clothes designers to put pockets back in women's dresses, skirts, and pants? I don't buy them unless pockets are in them, and I'm sure many women don't. Did you notice that I said WOMEN? Those little skinny, stretchy things don't fit us. I wonder if they ever wonder why a lot of their stuff is never sold. I bet it's the pockets.

Barbara J. Belisle

CHRISTIANITY

I am constantly befuddled by the absolute disregard of Christian teachings and beliefs exhibited in the media, in society, in the schools, in the homes—basically in every aspect of our daily lives. People claim to be Christians, and they scream "Bloody murder!" when some television show or killer or newly enacted law shows disrespect, abhorrence, or disbelief in the teachings of the Holy scriptures. Yet, these same people sit back and complain but allow only a few Christians to try to fight the system. Some groups even try to change Christian teachings to fit their personal beliefs, or they try to update them to fit modern times. How much more foolish will these people get? Can you imagine what it would be like if everyone who claimed to be a Christian would live their daily lives behaving like one?

America was established on the belief in Christianity. The country's laws are based on Christian teachings, and money (the root of all capitalism) announces proudly, "In God We Trust." America allows people from all over the world to come here and become citizens and worship as they please. That doesn't mean that America has to throw away its Christian beliefs and practices to show respect for other religious teachings. It is not disrespectful to other religious groups to have Christian signs, symbols, exhibitions, or programs in recognition of Christian beliefs and special periods that are celebrated by Christians. Also, if it doesn't conflict with another's belief, invite the other to participate, and if invited to, join the other in one of the celebrations he/she honors. And I don't understand all the fuss over prayer in the schools. Anyone can pray silently all day long, anytime. I do. God never said we have to pray aloud to be heard by Him. If a moment of silent meditation is set aside each day at the start of school or at any school event, what's wrong with that? Children of other faiths can also pray their prayer, and no one is disrespected.

America must reinstate and re-emphasize its Christian teachings, or the non-believers in high places and the mediocre in low places will turn America into a beautiful country filled with heathens and anarchists. God forbid.

HUH?

WHY SHOULD ACTORS AND ATHLETES BE PAID MILLIONS OF DOLLARS WHILE PEOPLE WITH SKILLS AND EDUCATION AND WHO WORK LONG HOURS DOING THINGS THAT ACTUALLY BENEFIT SOCIETY BE PAID LITTLE OR NOTHING????

Barbara J. Belisle

September 11, 2001, is not finished; "they" want to annihilate us. Stop politicking, profiteering, and reverting to the usual.

Barbara J. Belisle

THE UNTRAINED

I don't understand why the administrators of schools can't demand and get proper behavior from students and patrons who attend school-sponsored events-especially graduation exercises. There are some people-young people as well as grown-ups-who act like they have never been trained to be respectful during certain types of events. Graduation exercises are not football games; they're formal events honoring those who have accomplished an important goal that will effect the next phase in their lives. Screaming and whistling and guffawing should not be displayed nor tolerated. When the speaker requests that all applause be withheld until the last person or group has been acknowledged, then the request should be honored. There might come a time when security guards or policemen might have to be stationed in various areas with the power to escort the uncouth to outside. I hope it never comes to that.

Students who live in dormitories should not have to leave the building to find a quiet place to study. Loud noise should not be tolerated. Anyone who plays loud music and /or have noisy gatherings that disturb others should be evicted. Those who pay tuition-whether in a public or private institution-should have the right to sue the institution for not protecting their right to an appropriate environment for study. Also, those people who ride around campus with loud "music" blasting from their cars and parking-maybe not getting out of their cars-should be watched; who knows what their purpose is? A peaceful environment should be an accepted feature at any school. If students are told what is expected of them, conditions could easily change for the better.

Finally, will someone please tell those people with cell phones to turn them off before entering the church, the theater, and the library? Anyone who doesn't understand why I say this is an idiot and doesn't even need a phone!

WHAT I CALL GOOD TV

I am sick of talk-shows!! Why don't the cable television owners create a talk-show channel and put all of them in one place?? Give us the great games of old, the variety shows, informative interviews and visits to places around the world. There is always news somewhere in the world-show some of it! And please, CNN-Headline News, please give us the serious, established anchors again, instead of all of these young, pretty folks who sound like they're on talk shows discussing the movies and fashions. (Don't get me wrong-I like young, pretty people-just not reporting on serious matters as if they're talking to middle schoolers about the next sox-hop.)

Barbara J. Belisle

THE TEN COMMANDMENTS

The Ten Commandments should not be a political nor a judicial issue. It should be a personal issue used to evaluate one's words and actions each day. You see, I consider those laws to be rules to live by because you're human and must live with other humans on this earth. It doesn't matter what one's religion is or if one has no religion at all; he must co-exist peacefully with others. Anybody's God would want The Ten Commandments to be the law of the land because it tells us what to do in order to receive His approval. Basically, the laws tell us how to live right, and what's wrong with doing right?

Whether or not the Ten Commandments should be engraved in marble in the shape of a tablet and placed in a public building is now an issue on its way to a higher court. Why? Since we live in a country where the separation of church and state is the law of the land, then the marble monument should be placed in front of a church, in a park, in someone's yard, or somewhere else. If one lives the Ten Commandments, it's not necessary to put up flags, monuments, and posters to advertise the fact.

LAND

How many people have died and taken their land with them? How many rulers were buried with their domains? Land does not belong to anybody! Even the piece one is buried in is not his for long. Generations pass, and changes take place, and suddenly, there's a mall being built over you. One American poet once wrote, "There are more people in the ground than on it." Some of those people fought over land, and you see where they are now. For you and me, there will be no exception. My point is, why are people fighting over land / territory, when it doesn't belong to any of them? It doesn't make sense!

ABOUT THE AUTHOR

Barbara J. Belisle is a retired English teacher. While a teacher she received one of Alabama's first "Golden Apple for the Teacher" awards, was listed in "Who's Who Among America's Teachers," was selected as the "Teacher of the Year" at her school, and was presented the community service award.

She holds membership in three professional education associations, her local theater group, and the American Association of University Women. She works part time at Carmichael Library at the University of Montevallo. She has authored a short story collection, a children's story, and several personal narratives.

One of her poems, "Do Fence Them In," was published in the National Library of Poetry's "Windows of the Soul."

She is the mother of three, grandmother of six, and the great-grandmother of one.

www.ingramcontent.com/pod-product-compliance
Lightning Source LLC
Chambersburg PA
CBHW030359290526
45785CB00004B/1824